MUM

I'M A LUCKY DUCK!

MOM

I'M A LUCKY DUCK!

Bob Elsdale and Holly

Text by Patrick Regan

**Andrews McMeel
Publishing, LLC**

Kansas City • Sydney • London

in association with PQ Blackwell

FOR MY MUM

BEFORE
I WAS EVEN BORN,

YOU LOVED ME.

BEFORE YOU EVER SAW MY FACE...

YOU DREAMED OF A BRIGHT

FUTURE FOR ME.

YOU PROTECTED ME AND KEPT ME WARM.

AND THEN ONE DAY...

I ARRIVED...

—— ⚬⚬ ——

AND YOU WERE MY

EVERYTHING.

⚬⚬

WHERE YOU WENT,

I FOLLOWED.

WHAT YOU SAID,
I ECHOED.

EVERYTHING

I KNOW, I LEARNED FROM YOU.

WHEN I WAS AFRAID TO TRY

SOMETHING NEW...

A PEP TALK AND A GENTLE

NUDGE FROM YOU...

WERE ALL I NEEDED TO

DIVE IN!

AND WITH EACH RISK TAKEN,
A BIGGER WORLD
OPENED UP FOR ME.

NEW EXPERIENCES. NEW FRIENDS.

BUT ONE CONSTANT...

MY INCREDIBLE MUM!

YOU TAUGHT ME HOW TO CHERISH FRIENDSHIP...

BUT TO STAND ON MY OWN

TWO FEET.

YOU ENCOURAGED ME TO

FIND MY OWN WAY...

—— ——

BUT WHEN MY FEATHERS

WERE RUFFLED...

YOU WERE THERE TO

SMOOTH THEM.

SINCE THE DAY I WAS BORN,
YOU HAVE GIVEN ME YOUR

WISDOM AND EXPERIENCE.

THE BEST MUMS ARE
JUST LIKE THAT:

UNFLAPPABLE.

WITH EVERY LOVING ACT AND PATIENT LESSON,

YOU PREPARED ME FOR MY LIFE AHEAD.

YOU WERE ALWAYS THERE AT THE STARTING LINE,

DELIGHTING IN MY LITTLE TRIUMPHS.

IN OTHER WORDS, YOU GAVE ME WINGS.

[NOT TO MENTION A VERY ATTRACTIVE PAIR OF FEET!]

WELL, YOU MAY NOT REALISE IT, MUM,
BUT I'M JUST AS PROUD OF YOU.

SOMEDAY I HOPE TO REPAY YOU...

BUT FOR NOW, YOU CAN JUST

PUT IT ON MY BILL!

I KNOW I'VE STILL GOT A LOT
TO LEARN ABOUT LIFE,

BUT I DO KNOW
ONE THING FOR SURE...

I'M A LUCKY DUCK

TO HAVE A MUM
LIKE YOU!

THE END

*NO DUCKLINGS WERE HARMED IN THE MAKING OF THIS BOOK.

To create these images, my family and I incubated a group of ducklings at home. Despite having them arrive a day early, we ended up with eleven healthy little fluffballs who, like most babies, slept a lot for a day or so, then started to eat and eat and eat.

You can't train ducklings. You can only position them and keep taking photographs until you get what you want. In watching them carefully, it was obvious that, even at two days old, some were naturally bold, some timid and one or two were just real 'stars'. We worked with two sets of ducklings, and our animal handler brought 'Mum' in when needed. Dave 'The Hat' Broadbridge is such a charmer that his whispers seemed to work wonders, and his signature hat, an Australian leather bushman's affair, also came in handy, serving as a holding pen for up to three ducklings at a time.

The greatest challenge was to create a unique world that would showcase these cute little ducklings. So although no ducklings were harmed, several pillows were sacrificed in the building of 'Featherworld'. Our first attempt was way too soft, and the little yellow balls of fluff sank in so deeply that they could hardly be seen.

Apart from her very significant role in helping to conceptualise the book, my daughter Holly was responsible for duckling rotation and gently drying them with a hair dryer as they came off the water. I have long wanted to collaborate with her on a project, and she made a very unique contribution to this one.

I was amazed at just how much expression these little ducklings could show, and I think we've captured some really strong feelings and sentiments. It remains a great privilege to be able to spend time working with animals large and small: elephants, pigs, ducks . . . What next? I ask myself.

Bob Elsdale

ACKNOWLEDGEMENTS

I would like to thank the following for making this book possible:

Our little ducklings, who performed so diligently. They are now living out their natural lives on a beautiful lake in Surrey, England.

My daughter Holly, who worked with me as both assistant and art director. We conceptualised the book together, and her contribution was invaluable to the production process from start to end.

Patrick Regan, whose excellent text really embodies the concept of the book.

Dave 'The Hat' Broadbridge, who is a licenced animal handler for film and television. He has such a respect and love for all animals and never allows any of our subjects to become stressed when working in front of the camera.

Beth Manning at C.P. Hart, London, for kindly supplying the pedestal basin used on the set.

Finally, Geoff Blackwell and Ruth Hobday at PQ Blackwell, and Chris Schillig and Kirsty Melville at Andrews McMeel Universal, for their vital help in visualising the book.

Mom, I'm a Lucky Duck!

copyright © 2007 by Bob Elsdale Photography Ltd.
www.bobelsdale.com

This edition published in 2011 by Andrews McMeel Publishing, LLC, an Andrews
McMeel Universal company, 1130 Walnut Street, Kansas City, Missouri, 64106.

ISBN: 978-0-7407-7279-5
Library of Congress Control Number on file.

www.andrewsmcmeel.com

Produced and originated by
PQ Blackwell Limited
116 Symonds Street, Auckland,
New Zealand
www.pqblackwell.com

Book concept, photography, and digital art by Bob Elsdale
Text by Patrick Regan
Artwork design by Victoria Skinner
Jacket design by Carolyn Lewis

Printed by Everbest Printing International Ltd, China.